D1313752

A New Parrot

David Boruchowitz

T.F.H. Publications, Inc.
One TFH Plaza
Third and Union Avenues
Neptune City, NJ 07753

This book has been published with the intent to provide accurate and authoritative information in regard to the subject matter within. While every precaution has been taken in preparation of this book, the publisher and author assume no responsibility for errors or omissions. Neither is any liability assumed for damages resulting from the use of the information herein.

ISBN 0-7938-3079-6

Printed and bound in the United States of America

www.tfh.com

Printed and Distributed by T.F.H. Publications, Inc.
Neptune City, NJ

Contents

Parrots as Pets

All living things deserve our respect and protection, and pet parrots require no less. They may, however, require more—a great deal more. Long appreciated by parrot owners, the intelligence of these birds has recently been scientifically documented, and their talking ability, which for centuries has been thought to be mere mimicry, has been shown to be capable of engaging birds and humans in true communication. In fact, the Psittacines (parrots) and Corvids (crows, ravens, etc.) exhibit problem solving, learning, communicative, and tool-making skills that place them with dolphins and apes.

Add to this the fact that many of these species are either threatened or in decline—mainly due to habitat destruction—and it is clear that parrots deserve special attention and care. While any pet owner is under serious responsibility to provide for the animal, the parrot owner has taken on a particular challenge—to provide the best home possible for a special companion animal.

A parrot may not be a person, but neither is it a mindless, feathered automaton, and it should never be treated like one.

Owner Responsibility

The appeal of tame hookbills is almost universal; after all, few people can resist the charm of a bird that will sit on your arm and speak to you in English. Intelligent and affectionate, parrots are the perfect companion for many people, but they are not suited to everyone. Because they are sensitive and

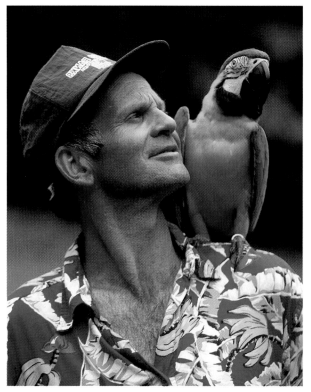

The appeal of parrots is obvious, but the decision to have one as a pet should not be taken lightly.

smart, they have emotional needs as well as physical ones, and because they are long-lived (the larger parrots have life spans similar to our own), they require a sustained commitment.

Is a tame parrot right for you? It is just as important to ask if you are right for a parrot. In this book you'll find the information you need to make these decisions, and to provide a loving, healthy, and happy home for one of these special birds. Perhaps you have already decided, or you may even have just brought your new friend home; in that case, this book will help you both begin to enjoy a lifetime together.

What Is a Parrot?

There is a great variety among the various species of parrots, and even among members of a given species, in size, color, shape, dietary needs, intelligence, talking ability, and "personality," but it is possible to lump all large parrots together and consider their general traits.

All parrots are Psittacine birds—the hookbills. This group also includes such birds as parakeets (or budgerigars), lorikeets, cockatiels, parrotlets, and lovebirds. All of these make fine pets, but this book will concentrate on the larger parrots and cockatoos.

As with any classification, this distinction is part imagined and part real, and size is not the only factor that links these birds together. While any short-tailed parrot about 12 inches in length would be considered a large parrot, there is a behavioral component as well. For example, the spunky little Senegal parrot, a multi-colored, gray-headed bird that is a close relative of the well-known African Grey parrots, is merely a handful, but in many ways it acts the same as its giant cousins and not at all like, say, the more similarly-sized Agapornis lovebird. One might be tempted to split off any bird with a long tail (defined as at least as long as the rest of the bird's body) as a "parakeet," but everyone would place the long-tailed macaws in with Amazons and cockatoos.

For the purposes of this book, we will mainly consider all birds that are generally agreed to be "large parrots." These are medium-to-large animals commonly called by the names "parrot," "cockatoo," and "macaw." Price-wise, they are collectively more expensive than small parrots and parakeets and in the price range of registered, purebred dogs.

What Kind of a Pet is a Parrot?

Anyone who loves animals will probably like birds, and any bird lover will probably enjoy owning a parrot. There are, however, many people who are not really the pet type, who would never want a canary or a budgie or a finch, but who love a parrot and cannot imagine living without it. What makes parrots so desirable?

The Bad News

Parrots are such delightful, amusing, and affectionate pets that once you get into a description of their positive qualities, you might be less likely to pay attention to the negative ones, and that can have disastrous results—for both you and the bird. If I had to choose one word to describe parrots, it would be strong. They are strong-minded, strong-willed, strong-hearted, strong-beaked, strong-voiced, strong-memoried, and they have strong preferences. This means that everything about them is extreme—their positive and their negative attributes.

Noise

The different species of parrots vary widely in how noisy they are. Some are so noisy, even by parrot standards, that certain other species will not breed if the loudmouths are in the same area. But all of them can and at least occasionally will "talk" or "squawk" or "call" or "yell," but it's really a *scream*. Even the "quiet" parrots can be very loud. This is a major consideration relative to family members and neighbors—and not just for apartment dwellers. Many parrots are loud enough to disturb people living in the house next door or across the street.

Of course, you can train a parrot not to scream all the time, and certain species seem silent next to others, but you must keep in mind that almost any large parrot is going to be capable of making some horrific noises, and sooner or later it probably will.

Destruction

Most parrots have beaks capable of crushing very hard seeds and nuts, and all of them are capable of splintering wood and shredding fabric with their beaks. In fact, parrots have to gnaw and shred and splinter to keep their beaks trim and fit. Many

Like other macaws, the hyacinths have large and powerful bills.
Photo courtesy of David Holzman, Palmforest Hyacinth Macaws, 5100 South Dixie Highway, Suite 13, West Palm Beach, FL 33405

The inquisitive nature of parrots is endearing, but it may also get them into trouble. Take care to monitor adventurous and risky behavior.

parrot owners place a piece of lava rock in their pet's cage for them to hone their bill against, and all parrots need to be permitted to chew on wood and other material. The largest parrots—the macaws and cockatoos—are even capable of escaping from welded wire pens by pulling the mesh apart. Many breeders of these birds resort to heavy metal nest boxes because the parrots turn a wooden one into splinters and sawdust before their brood is ready to leave the nest.

This means that any wood, fabric, plastic, or soft metal in the vicinity of your parrot is likely to be destroyed. Since the positive attributes of these birds encourage allowing them liberty in your home, at least part of the time, you must give serious thought to how and where you will house your pet. Allowing a parrot free time in a room full of antique furniture is asking for trouble.

Parrots are perfectly capable of biting; taming and establishing a trusting relationship will help to minimize, but probably not prevent, the risk of being hurt.

Not all of a parrot's nibbling and crushing is to keep its beak in shape. They also chew on things just for the fun of it. Parrots love toys—in fact they must have toys, but the birds often decide for themselves what looks interesting to play with. As with any intelligent animal, a parrot is easily bored, and boredom can lead to some significant vices, including wrecking anything it can. Parrots also chisel and split and pry apart things to look for food. After all, you never know, there might be a tasty treat hiding inside that table leg!

Danger and Risk

Parrots can be dangerous to you as well as to your home, and you and your home can pose a serious risk to a parrot. It is important to understand what sorts of limitations owning a parrot will place on you and your family before deciding to get one.

That powerful beak can be used to bite, and bite hard. Hand-raised parrots are extraordinarily tame and loving, but they are also fearless—they have none of a normal bird's timidity. I once asked a professional parrot breeder if she ever used hand-tame birds for breeding, and she said yes, but she had to be very careful because when a bird with no fear of humans gets the protective instincts of a nesting parrot, it is a potential danger. It is important that you stop and consider what a bird that can bite a broomstick in half could do to a finger, nose, or ear. To be sure, the vast majority of pet parrots have never bitten and will never bite anyone, and a little careful thought and preparation on your part can keep up this record.

Parrots can also pose a risk to asthmatics or to people with allergies. (The dusty nature of cockatoos' plumage is often more irritating to allergies than the dander from other parrots.) Before plunking down a fistful of cash and making room in your heart for a pet parrot, it would be a good idea to find out if you or anyone in your household is allergic. Borrow a bird for a couple of weeks if you have to, or find some other way of exposing everyone so that you can discover this type of problem before it creates a serious and difficult—not to mention heartbreaking—situation.

Parrots also can transmit diseases to humans, and vice versa, but if you buy a healthy bird and keep it in good health, that will not be a big concern. There is, however, a lot of folk "wisdom" out there about the hazards of having a bird in the house, so I mention this to indicate that this is one danger that you won't have to worry much about.

What about the risk to your pet from regular household situations? Do you have a two-year-old in your house? Did you ever? Remember what it was like? Parrots are perpetual two-year-olds. They are curious, mischievous, fun-loving, dexterous, smart, sometimes disobedient...and they can fly! They love to get into and behind and on top

A pet parrot, like this conure, can become very attached to its owner and will appreciate time spent together.

of and in between things. Anything new or different immediately attracts their attention. And, Murphy's Law of Animal Behavior applies double to them: if an animal can get into any kind of trouble, it will.

What about the bird itself? Pet parrots can meet injury and death in a seemingly endless variety of ways. They have been known to drown in an open toilet, be electrocuted by chewing through wires, hang themselves in window blind cords, fly into rotating fan blades, be killed by other pets, die from exposure to household chemicals, be poisoned by eating houseplants or from fumes from cooking utensils, and, of course, literally fly the coop.

The Good News

The foregoing was not meant to dissuade you from the idea of a pet parrot, only to put things into perspective so that you can evaluate their positive features honestly.

Sociality

Pet parrots are the best of all pet worlds, with the devotion of a puppy, the playfulness of a kitten, the intelligence of a monkey, and the sense of humor of a standup comic.

They are cuddly, loving, and affectionate to the extreme, and they love to play games, to play practical jokes, and to "help" their humans with their daily tasks.

Intelligence and Talking

The intelligence of parrots, long recognized by their owners, is now a matter of scientific study, and these birds have been shown to be extremely intelligent. Even aside from the obvious appeal of a bird that can actually use human language correctly, a parrot's mental abilities are yet another

The African Grey is commonly believed to be the most talented of the talking parrots and has been the subject of a great deal of research.

factor that help them integrate into a human family.

Although many parrot people are not too excited by performing birds, parrots can certainly learn to do tricks—even extremely complex ones. Performing parrots are trained to roller skate, sing duets with their trainers, play basketball, "mail" letters, and retrieve objects from people in an audience.

But it is the ideas that parrots come up with themselves that most endear them to their human family. It is not uncommon to find a parrot that calls the family dog in its master's voice and obviously delights in the animal's confusion when it obediently and expectantly arrives. Parrots easily learn to open cabinets and manipulate other household objects. They exclaim "Yum!" loudly when they see their food dish coming, and I've heard of one parrot, who was extremely unusual in dis-

The price of a parrot will be contingent upon a number of factors: availability, species, and whether it was hand-raised.

liking baths, who would warn, "Watch out!" whenever its owner prepared a bath for another of the household's parrots. People teaching their parrots have had the tables turned on them by the birds, which hold up an object in one foot and ask "What's this?" and then say "Good boy!" when the person answers correctly.

Dr. Irene Pepperberg's world-famous African Grey named Alex can correctly answer questions about objects, such as "how many?" "what color?" and "which is different?" He has even coined his own descriptive names for things in the same way that chimps taught sign language do; he called an apple a "banerry," combining the words "banana" and "cherry."

Longevity

Many dog and cat owners suffer a grievous loss when their pet ages and dies, even though it has lived a very long life for that species. With many species of large parrots and cockatoos, their owners are more concerned about providing for their pet in their wills than they are about losing their friend prematurely. Reliable data about parrot life spans is hard to find, but the smaller parrots certainly live 10 to 20 years at least, and the larger birds seem to live about as long as humans. Cases of birds 100 years old or more even exist.

Age should be considered when making the decision to own a parrot. These young green-cheeked conures may require more attention, but they will be ripe for taming.

How Much Does a Parrot Cost?

The initial cost of a parrot, though considerable, pales in comparison to the long-term maintenance costs. There are three principal ways in which adding a parrot to your home will impact your budget—initial cost, upkeep, and healthcare.

Prices

A parrot is expensive. As with purebred dogs, incredibly large sums of money change hands for the more sought after individuals, but even plain old Amazons or macaws are not inexpensive. Of course, a cockatiel can command thousands of dollars if it is one of the first sporting a new color mutation, but the average price for less unique members of that species is about $50. Parrots such as the ones we will be talking about in this book are normally in the price range of a few hundred to a few thousand dollars, with a few species being less, and a few being more. Within that range, there can be variation for individuals of a given species based on age, sex, taming/training, physical condition, and other factors. Geography has an effect, too; in Florida, for example, where there are many breeders of parrots, the same bird will bring considerably less than it would in New Hampshire or Wisconsin.

For these reasons, I will not be specifying "good" prices for these birds. It is more important for you to look for the best source for your bird—a reputable breeder or retailer will not be trying to fleece you, and any extra you pay for a bird from such an individual over some bargain-basement-priced bird is money very well spent. It is expensive to breed, raise, and hand tame these animals, and the adage that you get what you pay for is completely applicable.

Maintenance Costs

A healthy parrot has a healthy appetite, and the cost of proper food for the bird is not insignificant, though it certainly is less than that for most dogs. A parrot does not need ornate or elaborate housing, but it needs a large, safe, and clean cage to call home, even if it spends most of the day outside of it. A playpen or gym is not absolutely necessary, but it is the easiest and best way to provide for a parrot's needs for exercise and stimulation. One ongoing cost you may not be thinking of for a pet parrot is the cost of toys. Not only are parrots destructive of their toys, it is easier to design toys that the bird naturally destroys in the process of playing with them than it is to try to armor plate them in such a way that a parrot cannot disassemble them. And, being as bright and spoiled as a toddler, even quasi-indestructible toys will be cast aside on a regular basis in favor of something new and more interesting.

Medical Expenses

For parrots, as for any living thing, an ounce of prevention is worth a pound of cure. There is no reason to expect to have enormous veterinary bills for your pet parrot, but there is no reason to assume you will never have them.

You do not walk around each day, consumed with worry that you or a member of your family will come down with a dire disease or be critically injured in an accident, but any sane person recognizes that these are real possibilities and makes contingency preparations. Getting sufficient medical insurance is not a concern for the parrot owner, but possible veterinary bills are, since the other major component of reasonable preparation for medical emergencies applies to parrots as well as people, and that is finding a reliable doctor and going regularly for checkups, tests, and vaccinations.

Your Vet

The care of exotic birds is a specialty, and most veterinarians are not trained in it. There is, however, a growing number of avian veterinarians, certified in the treatment and care of exotic birds, especially parrots. It is important to find one in your area, and then to take your parrot to him or her when you get it, and regularly thereafter.

Checkups

At a regular checkup the veterinarian will check the bird's vital signs, weight, plumage, and overall health. The doctor will also develop a relationship with you and with your parrot, which is important in the event that the bird does become ill.

What Does a Parrot Need?

A pet parrot needs a safe cage, toys and play area, a healthy diet, and a stress-free, loving, stimulating environment. If you can provide these, you can properly care for your bird.

How Much Time Does a Parrot Require?

If this book were being written by a parrot, the answer to this question would probably be "All of your time." Remember that parrots are flock birds, and that you and your family are your bird's "flock." A parrot is not a good choice for a household in which everyone is gone during the day, though some people find that leaving the television on for their bird helps counteract the loneliness. In a multi-parrot household, however, birds whose cages are near each other can keep themselves happy while the humans are gone, if they are free to come out and socialize all evening.

Of course, the time you spend with your parrot is enjoyable to you, too, and much of it can simply be you doing what you have to do and the parrot interacting with you much as a young child playing in the same room where a parent is working or relaxing. In any case, the decision to purchase a parrot requires a sincere commitment of substantial amounts of time. If you do not have the time to give but still want to enjoy a parrot, a much better choice would be to get one or more breeding pairs that are not hand-tame. They won't come out and snuggle and play with you, but neither will they expect you to spend time with them.

Selecting a Parrot

Having decided a parrot is right for you, how do you go about choosing one? Taking the first bird you find available is not likely to get you the perfect match. So far, we've been talking in general terms about "parrots." This chapter contains some information about the various types of parrots in order to give you a feel for the differences among them.

Once you have in mind the type(s) of parrots you would like to share your home with, you'll need to know how to go about finding an individual bird. Of course, it is very common for someone to make up their mind about which species of parrot they want and then to go into a pet store and fall in love with a totally different parrot. The best parrot for you is the one that you choose—and the one that chooses you.

Sex

Although some people feel that male parrots make the best talkers, one of the best talking parrots I have ever seen was a female Amazon. Ask the owner of a female parrot about this and you're likely to get one of two answers. Either you will be told that females speak as well as males, or you will hear that any lack of speaking ability is made up for by the affectionate personality of a hen parrot. In other words, males might be slightly better talkers on average, but parrots of both sexes make wonderful pets.

The only other factor to consider is that females can become eggbound (see the chapter on health for details). I know of people who have lost a beloved pet to this condition and refuse ever to purchase another female bird. Fortunately, it is not very common for a pet hen to become eggbound.

Size

Parrots come in all sizes, from birds that can sit three in your palm to large macaws and cockatoos that will weigh down your arm. Size, however, is not closely related to noisiness, talking ability, or trainability.

With large parrots suitable for a single companion pet, it is safe to say that the biggest factor concerning the actual size of the bird will be the size (and expense) of the cage needed. The largest parrots are also the most destructive and need the sturdiest, heaviest cages.

As for relative harmlessness, I have seen 5-inch lovebirds that were savage biters and 3-foot macaws that were as cuddly and sweet as a kitten. Obviously, though, a savage macaw can do a lot more damage. Pick the kind of parrot you want, and if size is important to you, then select a species from the size group you want.

Color

Should you pick a parrot because of its color? Sometimes people are taken by a particular color pattern. Certainly many female eclectus parrots have been chosen by an initial amazement at their coloration, then later their wonderful personality comes through, and people begin to appreciate the beauty and desirability of the drabber males.

Large parrots such as macaws tend to be expensive; they also entail the added expense of a large, sturdy cage.

All parrots have great beauty when they are in good feather—there isn't an ugly duckling in the group. Since choosing a parrot is usually a matter of the two of you hitting it off from the start, color doesn't normally figure in very greatly. If, however, you wish to select a species and then go looking for an individual to purchase, use any parameters you wish to make that choice.

Not-So-Basic Green

The default color for parrots is green, but very few parrots leave it at that; in fact, a solid green parrot is a rarity. The big green group is, of course, the Amazons, but color highlights are such a trademark for these birds that most of their common names derive from the particular color they have and its location: yellow-naped, lilac-fronted, orange-winged, blue-cheeked, blue-faced, red-tailed, double yellow-headed, blue-fronted, etc. (In these names "front" refers to the forehead area.)

Shyne Browne, who dedicated her life to the gentle blue hyacinth macaws.
Photo courtesy of David Holzman, Palmforest Hyacinth Macaws, 5100 South Dixie Highway, Suite 13, West Palm Beach, FL 33405

Basic Black and White

Parrots seem unable to make a simple fashion statement. Many cockatoos are overall black or white, but the black species tend to have red accents, and among the white ones, many have yellow or pink highlights or overwashes or both. With or without other colors, the restrained beauty of these white and black birds is indisputable.

Not-So-Subtle Grey

The African Grey is an overall gray color, but even without the red tail feathers it would be understatedly described in those terms. The beauty of these animals comes largely from the shadings and contrasts it manages without the use of bright colors. Even the red tail is not gaudy, but rather a maroon or crimson.

Shameless Show-Offs

Some parrots simply insist on making a fashion statement—a loud one. I've already mentioned the red and purple female eclectus parrot, but there are others such as the sun conure, which is notable for its bright and contrasting color pattern.

Temperament

Some parrots are active and noisy, others much more sedate and quiet. There are no generally nasty species, but some, like the Goffin's cockatoo, are known for being exceptionally loving babies. But the biggest difference among species of parrots is probably in their overall noisiness. Some twitter and chirp, others screech raucously. Some cluck and squawk and grumble, others scream incessantly. Within a given species, there is a great variation in how much noise a bird will make.

If talking ability is an important criterion for your new pet parrot, consider an African Grey or one of the Amazons.

Even given a single bird, there will be considerable difference in how noisy it is in different settings and contexts. A bird that has learned to screech in order to get people's attention can usually be trained not to make such a racket by a patient person who will refuse to acknowledge it when it screams but who attends to all of its needs the rest of the time. Rest assured of two fast rules: yelling at a bird only escalates the argument, and one bird plus one bird usually equals a lot more than twice the noise.

Talking Ability

The extent to which parrots can learn to mimic and talk varies greatly, and not just from species to species. Some birds are just better talkers than others. Species-wise, the best bet for a good talker is one of the Amazons, an African Grey, or a large cockatoo, though many macaws also do very well. Even species that are not considered talkers, however, often respond to diligent and tireless training.

Fortunately, there is a pretty foolproof way of buying a talker—select a bird already talking. By the time it is weaned, a talking parrot can already say several words, perhaps whistle a tune, and obey a few commands. Although a non-talking bird may simply reflect a lack of time spent teaching it, any bird that is already talking certainly is likely to continue to learn.

Finding Your Bird Through a Reputable Breeder/Store

As a responsible pet owner, you must do everything within your power to avoid supporting the illegal trade in exotic birds. Every contraband parrot that winds up for sale somewhere represents many other parrots that died packed into duffle bags, or drugged, or worse. The easiest way to avoid this black market is also the easiest way to get the best possible pet you can—buy only a close-banded,

Although cockatoos do not exhibit the bright colors of many of the macaws and Amazons, the colored crests and subtle highlights can be quite attractive.

hand-fed, tame baby parrot from a reputable source.

The vast majority of people in the pet bird trade are dedicated, honest, and trustworthy. Unfortunately, wherever there is money to be made, there will be those few who ruin things. A reputable bird dealer will be happy to supply references and documentation, and you should not hesitate to ask for these.

Taming and training are ideal ways to spend time with a pet parrot, but be certain that this time is enjoyed by both of you.

A Written Guarantee

As with any large purchase, a written guarantee is a good idea; again, reputable dealers are happy to give one, plus veterinarian records.

Close-Banding

Seamless bands are placed on a chick's foot while it is still in the nest. A few days later, the band can no longer fit over the toes and is permanently on the leg. These bands often contain the hatch year and other information identifying the breeder. They also provide a check against written records such as vaccination or sexing documents.

Microchipping

The process of microchipping birds has gained popularity. A tiny device is implanted under the skin of the bird, and for the rest of its life it is easily identifiable by simple scanning equipment, similar to the way in which a credit card can be swiped to identify an account.

DNA Testing

DNA testing is a very reliable method of determining the sex of birds, and since most parrots show no external differences between the sexes, it is very popular among parrot breeders. The test requires only a drop of blood or a plucked feather. A document with a band number will verify the sex of the bird in question.

Disease Testing and Vaccinations

There are various diseases detectable by blood test, and several diseases that can be vaccinated against. The veterinarian records for your baby parrot should include evidence of these. Because it is a good idea for you to find an avian veterinarian *before* you purchase your parrot, your doctor can detail these for you.

Parrot Housing

With two rare exceptions that are not found in the pet trade, all parrots are diurnal, meaning they are active by day and retreat to a safe roost for the night. No matter how active or busy their day is, they need a safe, comfortable and comforting, quiet, private, personal place to spend the night. This instinct has nothing to do with human habits, and your pet parrot will follow it as well.

Many pet parrots are not caged, at least while their owners are at home, but they each *have* a cage, which is typically left open while they are at liberty so that they can return to it if they desire. And they will return, not only to eat, but also just to hang out in a restful, non-challenging, non-threatening place. I remember a tourist attraction I visited that had over a hundred free-flying macaws and yet each had its own individual cage to which it returned each night.

A Suitable Cage

How big a cage do you need? Even experienced parrot breeders will argue over minimum cage sizes. However, when you get to the bottom of it, you'll find that those advocating the smallest cages rarely lock their birds in, so it actually boils down to a question of what the cage is going to be used for.

Flight Cages

If your pet will be kept in its cage for a significant portion of time, the cage must be large enough to allow proper exercise. Parrots are much more climbers than fliers, and they therefore utilize all six (in a rectangular cage) sides of the cage. Nevertheless, the cage must be long and wide enough to allow the bird to fly unimpeded, and should have a sturdy perch at each end so that the bird

An important factor when choosing a bird is the size of cage it will need. Be certain that your home has the proper location and space your bird requires.

may fly back and forth. Toys should be placed in such as way as not to present either a hazard or an obstruction to the bird's flight.

Because of their penchant for climbing, parrots can be housed comfortably in cages that are relatively much smaller than for other species of birds. For example, I prefer to keep finches, which are extremely high-strung and active little birds, in cages at least four feet long, and I never keep them in anything under two feet long. The same size cage, however, is suitable for a much larger cockatiel, or even a small parrot, since these birds are both less active and more inclined to clamber than fly around.

The height of the cage is significant especially for the long-tailed species like macaws. A cage insufficiently high will quickly result in the destruction of those beautiful tail plumes, which will become a dirty, frayed mess in no time. A suitable cage for the largest parrots—macaws and cockatoos—will be of walk-in size.

Liberty Cages

What if your bird's cage is going to be left open and you are going to let it out whenever you're at home? In this case, cage dimensions can be smaller. If anything, a smaller sleeping cage contributes to the bird's sense of privacy and retreat.

The size of such a cage is dictated mainly by the size and type of bird you have. The parrot should be able to sit on the perch (there is typically just one, in the center) without its tail or head hitting the cage bars, top, or bottom. For macaws, this means a very tall cage, and for cockatoos, the perch must be placed to give plenty of headroom for the fully spread crest.

Toys come in all shapes, sizes, and even flavors. Experiment with a many as possible until you find the best choice for your pet.

The bird should be able to *fully* extend and exercise its wings. There is no excuse for keeping a bird in a cage in which it cannot spread its wings all the way—it is the equivalent of your being in a straightjacket all day. Parrots often exercise by flying in place—beating their wings rapidly and either hanging on to the perch with their feet or simply hovering right above it. Such exercising behavior is not only an artifact of being in a cage too small for sustained flight, since they will occasionally do this in larger cages and even when loose, but the absolute minimum cage size must permit this behavior unrestricted.

Cage Accessories

Besides toys, a cage needs food and water bowls. Unfortunately, parrots are experts at dumping most of these. There are locking cups that can only be removed by unlocking them outside the cage, and these save a lot of mess and wasted food.

Perches should be sturdy and easily replaced—the birds will whittle them constantly. A variety of shapes and sizes promotes healthy feet.

Stands and Playpens

Parrots enjoy play stands of all types. There are many available, both freestanding and those that attach to the top of the cage. Or, if you're so inclined, you can let your imagination run wild with a homemade version. Perches, swings, ladders, and toys all contribute to a fun and healthy environment for your bird. Many parrots amuse themselves for hours on these gyms.

Cage Hygiene

You need to be aware of two facts: 1) birds are messy; 2) cages need to be kept clean.

The time-honored method of keeping a birdcage clean is still one of the best—a fresh sheet of newspaper on the cage bottom each day. Not only does it make cage hygiene quick and easy, it enables you to take note each day of your bird's droppings. Very often the first sign of illness in a bird is a change in the color or texture of its droppings.

A bird's feathers may become ragged or frayed if its cage is not large enough to allow it to spread its wings completely.

Larger cages that allow a bird to exercise and even fly around may be necessary for a large parrot that will remain in its cage for extended periods of time.

There is a lot of controversy concerning the various litters available for use in birdcages. They certainly cut down on labor, but they have been implicated in some fatal impactions of the digestive system. If your cage has a wire bottom far enough above the litter pan that a bird cannot reach its beak into the litter, these absorbent materials are suitable, though you will not be able to keep track of the bird's droppings with them.

The other important aspect of cage hygiene involves food and water cups. These should be positioned to minimize bird droppings falling into them, and they must be cleaned daily. The easiest way to keep up with this task is to have two sets of dishes. Every day a clean set can replace the dirty ones, which can be removed and washed.

Bedtime Buddies?

If you have more than one parrot, should you have more than one cage? Most parrots are highly social,

Food and water cups can easily become contaminated by bird droppings. Choose a cage that has properly placed food and water containers.

and it is common for them to come together in flocks of hundreds or even thousands of birds except when they are breeding. Parrots raised together or who are longtime friends usually get along well even when of different species, but in most cases they should each have their own cage. The cages can be next to each other for socializing purposes, but they should be separate. Mated pairs, on the other hand, often insist on remaining together even outside the breeding season, and you can usually detect them in wild flocks by the way they stay as a pair. However, even mated pairs need to be watched.

If for no other reason, the value of a pet parrot should normally dictate separate cages. Parrots can occasionally be very

Smaller parrots and setups may be more appropriate for pet owners who live in apartments or have limited space.

Caged birds are not particularly neat and tidy, so consider a cage's design in terms of cleaning and hygiene.

vicious toward each other. Sometimes, one member of a mated pair will severely injure or even kill its mate. The incidence of aggression is much higher among unmated birds, and it reaches its peak with rival birds. These can be breeding rivals—two birds of the same sex that see each other as contenders, or simply rivals for your attention. Like a toddler that tries to get on its parent's lap whenever the parent holds the new baby, multiple pet parrots will vie to be first on your list, and they can get quite nasty about it.

In the wild, a bird that is savaged by another can usually escape, flying miles away if necessary to avoid another attack. In a cage, this is obviously not possible, and the instinctive behaviors and appeasement gestures that normally limit serious aggression can be overwhelmed by the birds' enforced proximity.

Food and Nutrition

There are probably more misconceptions about the proper diet for a parrot than anything else. Many people think you simply feed a bird birdseed, but this is incorrect. Yes, many seeds can be a nutritious part of a parrot's diet, but they are neither necessary nor sufficient to keep your bird healthy. In other words, many parrots live perfectly healthy lives and *never* get seeds to eat, but no parrot can remain healthy if it gets *only* seeds to eat. This may be the most important fact you take away with you from this book.

Seeds are a natural part of a parrot's diet, but depending on the species and the locale, they may be only a small part. For example, there are no grainfields in the Amazon jungle, yet the area supports many thousands of parrots in dozens of species. Vegetation of all kinds makes up the bulk of their food intake, and they also eat some animal material, from insects to eggs, small animals to carrion.

So what *do* you feed a parrot? Well, although it is also an oversimplification, the idea that you feed a parrot foods that are also good for you is certainly a more accurate rubric than feeding it seeds. The key to a healthy diet for a parrot (or for almost any animal, including humans) is variety. Even for species whose nutritional needs have been studied in detail, there are undoubtedly holes in our knowledge, and many parrot species commonly kept as pets have not been researched much at all. A wide variety of wholesome foods will provide all of the major, minor, and trace elements needed for health, strength, and growth. This variety should include vegetables, grains, fruits, and an occasional source of some animal protein, and it should not be heavy on salt, sugars, or fats. There are three basic regimens that will provide your pet with a wholesome diet—pellet based, seed based, and neither based.

Nutrition is key to your pet's good health. When obtaining young parrots, be certain to find out about their previous eating habits.

Pellets

Many years ago, when people started realizing the inadequacies of an all-seed diet for parrots, pellets touted as a complete diet for birds started appearing on the market. The quality and variety available have grown over time, so today you have a choice of many different types and formulations. Some minor controversies have also grown, and today many people no longer consider it appropriate to feed *only* pellets. Their concerns include vitamin overdose, excess iron, food colors, and incomplete nutrition. It actually isn't important if any of these concerns are valid, since we can dismiss the entire problem simply by citing the obvious concern of boredom.

Imagine having your favorite food three times a day. Every day. Every week. Every month. Every year. Imagine always eating food that was crunchy—or that was mushy. Or food that was always dry—or slimy. Or food that was sweet—or tart, or bland, or spicy. Well, why do that to your parrot?

Variety is the spice of life, even for birds. Seeds, pellets, and fresh fruits and vegetables should all be a part of your parrot's diet.

So, forget worrying about whether "complete" diets really are complete. All of the major brands and types of pelletized parrot feed reflect a lot of time and money in researching the birds' nutritional requirements and formulating blends of ingredients that meet those needs very closely and perhaps totally. Therefore, you can rely on them to provide a healthy, wholesome base for a complete and appetizing diet. Supplement the pellets with fresh vegetables, fruits, and treats, and your pet will be happy and healthy.

Pellets are available in a variety of sizes, though even the smallest parrot can easily crack off a mouthful from the largest pellet, so size is more a matter of convenience—both yours and the bird's. The advantages of a pellet-based diet include ease of feeding, reliability, high nutritive value, lack of harmful or

Don't forget about fresh water; bowls and drinkers can become contaminated and must be changed and washed frequently.

Your parrot must always have a supply of food at its disposal. Check that seed hoppers and food containers are filled with fresh food every day.

"junk" ingredients, and extremely low waste; when each pellet is the same as the next, birds have little motivation to toss aside dozens of them, looking for that perfect morsel the way they often do with seed mixes. When you factor in these considerations, pellets are probably cheaper than seed mixes, especially when you realize that parrots hull all seeds, which means that a good part of what you are buying with seed mixes is waste, while pellets are 100 percent edible.

Seeds

Although a diet of only seeds is not healthy for parrots, seeds can be a welcome addition to a parrot's diet. A good illustration would be wheat as a complete diet for you. Humans can live a long time on nothing but wheat, but with decreasing health. Wheat provides a lot of vitamins,

minerals, energy, and fiber, and it can be consumed in a variety of ways—sprouted, cooked as a cereal, or ground for bread flour. It also has considerable protein. The amino acid profile of that protein, however, is not very good for growth, so children will be the first to show a deficiency on an all-wheat diet. It wouldn't take much to turn an all-wheat diet into a very wholesome (if tiring) diet—the additions could be as simple as milk, orange juice, and margarine, or legumes, eggs, and parsley, etc. So, what does it take to turn a seed mix into a healthy parrot diet? Well, first let's look at the mix itself.

Seed mixes are often a healthy combination of assorted seeds, dried vegetables, and dried fruits.

Seed Mixes

Fortunately, most commercial seed mixes are either more balanced than mixes in the past or they make it clear that they are a supplement and should not be the sole mixture provided. It may surprise you to know that large parrots enjoy and benefit greatly from eating a standard budgie mix of small millet and canary seeds. In fact, that diet is a vast improvement over straight sunflower seeds, since it is much lower in fat and higher in nutrition.

A very good basic diet for large parrots can be provided by feeding both a standard budgie mix and a mix of larger seeds made specifically for parrots. It is a good idea to go lightly on the sunflower seeds, which, though a favorite of parrots, contribute to obesity and fatty liver disease in relatively inactive pet birds. Some formulations leave these seeds out entirely and substitute safflower, which is also a favorite but with less fat. It is best to serve the two seed mixes in separate bowls,

Young cockatoos, like these four-week-old Goffin's, have special nutritional needs; consult your avian veterinarian or breeder for guidance.

Seed treats, especially millet sprays, are the favorite of many parrots. However, it's important that your pet eat its regular food as well.

both to eliminate waste and to monitor the bird's intake. If it starts leaning too heavily on the larger seeds, that bowl can be left empty for a while to encourage the bird to finish the others; this is rarely necessary, however, because parrots usually are quite fond of the small seeds as well.

Very often, parrot mixes also include treats such as dried vegetables and fruits; dried chili peppers appeal to almost all parrots, and they avidly consume them, hot flesh and fiery seeds alike.

Although there is some uncertainty as to whether it is nutritionally necessary to supplement a pellet diet, there is not the slightest doubt that it is necessary to supplement a seed diet. Such a diet does not contain all of the vitamins, minerals, and proteins that your bird requires.

Besides fresh fruits and vegetables, you can supplement a seed-based diet with cooked beans and grains, scrambled or hard-boiled eggs, low-fat cheeses, and cooked lean meat such as chicken. If you stay away from salty and greasy foods, almost anything in your kitchen will make a good treat for your parrot.

Seeds, although they should not be a parrot's sole source of food, can be an important part of a nutritious diet.

Seeds and Beans

Millions of humans subsist on diets that are basically seeds (grains) and beans (legumes), whether it be the tofu and rice of the Orient, the millet and peanuts of Africa, or the maize and beans of the Native Americans. Your parrot can also do very well on a diet with the same basis.

There are many commercially available mixes of this type that you cook and serve,

but you can make up any mixture of grains, rice, beans, and peas. If you cook up a batch, you can freeze single-serving portions to be thawed at feeding time.

Seed Treats

Probably the most universally accepted treat for pet birds is millet spray. There is something about millet on the stem that excites almost all birds, large and small. Birds that receive no seeds on a regular basis often find a bowl of mixed seeds a treat as well.

People Food

Many birdkeepers call a diet based on neither pellets nor seeds a "people food" diet, but foods that are good for you are generally good for your parrot. One of the greatest benefits of such a diet is that your bird will learn to accept anything you offer as food. It will have preferences—likes and dislikes—but it will not view something new in its bowl as the poisoned threat that so many parrots raised on just seeds will.

The Basics

Plants should make up the bulk of your bird's diet. Cooked and uncooked vegetables of all kinds are fine, as are cooked grains and legumes. Small amounts of egg, cottage cheese, or lean meat will supply necessary nutrients. Fruits are an excellent source of vitamins and are well liked by most parrots.

Be certain that fruits and vegetables are thoroughly washed of any harmful chemicals.

You should note that there is controversy surrounding avocados. Some breeders claim they are toxic to parrots, while others deny this. To play it safe, keep the guacamole away from your bird.

Sharing Your Table

Parrots often wind up at the family dinner table. This is a natural result both of the way in which these birds worm their way into people's hearts and of the fact that they are highly social birds (eating is a social function for them). Whether you choose to allow this is up to you, but you should realize that if you do, your bird will soon commandeer the entire meal and protest loudly if restrained from doing so. If allowed, it will move happily from plate to plate, sampling this and that.

However, it's not a good idea to allow them to have alcoholic or caffeinated beverages, or to pig out on junk food or heavy fried foods—as I said before, food that is good for you is good for your bird.

Cooking for Your Parrot

Many people make it a point to serve their parrots warm, home-cooked meals. Much more important than the temperature of the food is its quality and nutritional value, and home-cooked recipes usually abound in this department. Most prevalent

Whether served as a treat or as part of a meal, fresh fruits of all kinds will be relished by your parrot.

are recipes for "birdy bread," a whole-grain quick bread with tasty additions. Almost any whole-grain bread, however, makes wonderful parrot food. The only caution regarding such meals for your parrot is that you not leave them around too long. Two or three hours after feeding, the bowl should be removed and washed to prevent bacterial growth.

Lories

There was a time when I would have advised that your first parrot should never be a lorie. These spectacular and gorgeous birds have dietary needs based on nectar. As you might imagine, even if you had no problem supplying such a diet, the hygienic difficulties of keeping such a bird were substantial! There are available now, however, lorie diets that are pelletized.

Your Parrot's Good Health

It's important to have a good working relationship with an avian veterinarian, and such is neither developed nor fostered if you try to diagnose and treat your bird's ailments by yourself. Instead of giving details about major diseases, we'll cover common, everyday situations that do not necessarily require professional attention while making it very clear when you should seek the help of an avian veterinarian.

Is It Serious?

Even talking parrots can't tell you what's wrong with them, but there are reliable signs when they are ill. You will probably be able to tell something is wrong simply by a change in the bird's behavior. If the change is serious enough, waste no time in getting the bird to a qualified veterinarian.

Any bird that will not eat or drink will need medical care, even if just to rehydrate it. If your bird's breathing is audible—that is, if it makes rasping, clicking, or bubbly sounds, it needs to see the veterinarian. If your bird is fluffed up, with its feathers standing out, it is probably cold. If there is no reason for it to be cold and if it does not return to normal shortly after being placed in a warm, cozy spot, you should contact your veterinarian. Unusual lumps, bumps, or lesions anywhere on your bird warrant professional examination.

Basic First Aid

Minor wounds can be treated with an antiseptic and watched for signs of infection. Occasionally a wing feather will get broken. Left alone, it will remain until the next molt, but if you grasp it at

The more time an owner spends with a pet, the easier it is to spot any symptoms of ill health. The owner should pay close attention to the parrot's behavior and not hesitate to call a vet if anything appears wrong.

the base and pluck it out, it will regrow in a couple of months. Birds actually have remarkable immune systems and power of recuperation. Cuts and scrapes and bruises usually heal very quickly and without incident.

A bird that sits with its feathers fluffed out for no apparent reason should be closely monitored for health problems.

Wing Clipping

There are many arguments about the practice of wing clipping. At the one extreme are concerns of injury and escape with fully flighted birds; at the other are objections about interfering with a bird's natural movement. You will have to make your own decision.

An unclipped bird can fly away from dangers, even imagined ones or through open windows. It can also fly into ceiling fans, boiling pots, open flames, and closed windows. On the other hand, a clipped bird can hurt itself in a fall, cannot get away from marauding animals, and cannot exercise its normal behavior.

There is a compromise of sorts—clipping only one wing. This restricts a bird's ability to simply fly off but enables it to still have the capability of flight. Unfortunately, it also compromises all the benefits of both extremes. A partially clipped bird can partially fly away from dangers, through open windows, into ceiling fans, boiling pots, open flames, and closed windows; it can partially hurt itself in a fall, partially get away from marauding animals, and partially exercise its normal behavior.

This is an emotional argument. Personally, I feel that keeping a fully flighted bird in a cage in which it is unable to make a sustained flight is not much different from clipping its wings—in either case the bird must resort to climbing to get around. And, it is true that even in the wild, parrots do a lot of "three-handed" climbing with both feet and the beak.

A parrot given liberty in a human's home faces adventures and dangers that make free flight both advantageous and disadvantageous. If you intend to take your parrot outdoors, or if you will be traveling with it, wing clipping is almost mandatory. It is an enormous risk to move your parrot outside your home if it is unclipped.

If you decide to clip, use a pair of sharp scissors. Extend the wing, and trim the flight feathers about halfway down their length. Leave the last few uncut so that the bird looks normal with the wings folded. If the bird still has too much flight ability, you can cut the feathers down a bit more.

Wing clipping, a hotly debated topic amongst many bird keepers, is a matter of personal preference for owners.

Wing clipping is usually the best way to prevent a parrot from flying away outdoors.

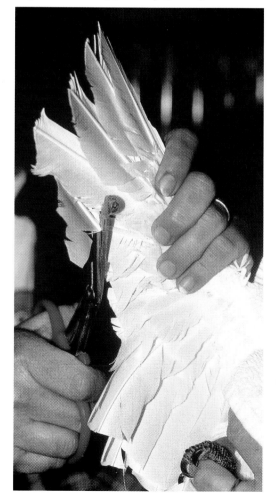

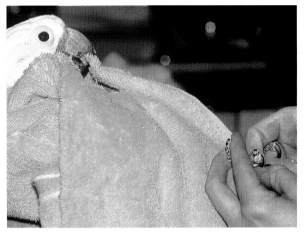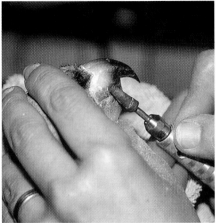

Although most owners can master the art of nail clipping, beak shaping is best left to a vet.

The procedure is like a haircut for you; except for the shaft right against the body, a feather is dead material and insensitive to pain. The clipping will need to be repeated every year after the bird molts.

Nail Trimming and Beak Shaping

Wild parrots usually keep their nails and beaks trim by climbing and gnawing. Domesticated birds occasionally need a bit of help. Have the person from whom you buy your parrot show you how to clip its nails properly.

Abrasive materials like concrete perches and lava rocks placed in their cages are useful, and birds will chew on them to wear their beaks down. If you feel that your parrot's beak is becoming over-

Household dangers such as fumes, chemicals, and drafts should be considered when situating your new parrot in your home.

grown, it is a simple procedure for your veterinarian to trim it. Sometimes a bird will have a chronic problem with an overgrown beak. If the bird is tractable so that you can work on it alone, you can ask your veterinarian to show you how to keep it trim.

Fumes

All birds are extremely sensitive to toxic vapors. Paints, varnishes, cleaning products, and other common household chemicals can be quickly lethal to your parrot. You usually have little or no warning, with a bird dying in a matter of minutes.

A very common cause of death in pet birds is non-stick cookware. The instructions that come with these pans usually say you should never heat them empty. The reason for this is that the non-stick coating, when heated past a certain point, gives off a gas that is extremely dangerous, and birds will drop dead from concentrations that won't even affect you. Even if you never intend to heat such a pan empty, there is always the chance of a pot of food boiling dry, with the same effect. If you have a bird, and if you must use non-stick cookware, make sure that the pans are never allowed to heat dry. Recently, concern has also been raised about similar hazards from plastic cooking bags.

So many common household chemicals are dangerous or lethal to birds that there are Internet sites listing them, and these are constantly updated. The safest thing is to assume that

Fresh air and sunshine can be a great boost to a parrot's health.
Photo courtesy of David Holzman, Palmforest Hyacinth Macaws, 5100 South Dixie Highway, Suite 13, West Palm Beach, FL 33405

Feather plucking is a serious habit that can be very difficult to break. Consult your avian vet at the first sign of a problem.

any cleaning or cosmetic product is dangerous, unless the manufacturer specifically states that it was tested on birds—not just on "pets" or "animals," since they often neglect birds under these categories.

Poisonous Plants

Many common houseplants are poisonous, including *Dieffenbachia*, poinsettias, ivy, and others. If you have houseplants where your parrot can get to them, you must be certain that they are not toxic. Your bird, however, will most likely destroy any plant you have, poisonous or not, so houseplants are not a good idea with a parrot in any case.

Parasites

In a biological sense, parasites are the most successful forms of life, and creatures like people and parrots exist to serve as their hosts. Such a view, of

Certain ailments may only be detected by a vet; therefore, regular checkups should be scheduled.

course, is unacceptable to people and parrots. While wild birds face many parasitic threats, pet birds do so less commonly, and all of them can be dealt with rather easily.

Mites and Lice

Although your parrot won't trade fleas with the family dog or cat, there are ectoparasites that afflict them equally. Besides the discomfort they cause your pet, these insects and arachnids drain a bird's strength and health with their bloodsucking, and they spread diseases.

Like a pet with fleas, a bird with an infestation of parasites may be constantly scratching. Not an occasional itch, or the blissful head and neck scratching almost all pet parrots love to get from their owners. Some infestations will only be manifest if you observe the creatures themselves or their debilitating effect on your bird's health.

As you play with your pet, you should be in the habit of checking it for signs of disease, parasites, wounds, or unusual growths. And, of course, you should be aware of changes in its behavior that might indicate a medical problem. Your veterinarian will also examine your bird for evidence of mites or lice during routine checkups.

Air Sac Mites

These insidious creatures set up house in the tiny air sacs in a bird's respiratory system. They can quickly build up populations that are dangerous to your bird's health. Your veterinarian will be able to diagnose and treat these easily.

Scaly Leg

The mite that causes this affliction burrows under the scales of the legs and feet of a bird, causing the scales to distend and become encrusted. It can also affect the face, generally around the beak. This can often be treated simply by smearing grease (vegetable shortening, petroleum jelly, etc.) liberally on the affected area. This suffocates the offending creatures. If this is unsuccessful, your veterinarian can prescribe a stronger treatment.

Cuttlefish bone can be an important supplement to a parrot's diet, especially a bird that suffers from a calcium deficiency.

Internal Parasites

Gastrointestinal worms are usually more of a problem in poultry than in pet parrots, but if you suspect them due to changes in your bird's stools or chronic loss of weight, your veterinarian can identify the culprits, if present, from a stool sample and then prescribe treatment.

Respiratory Problems

The first step in preventing respiratory problems is in keeping your bird healthy, with plenty of fresh vegetables, proper temperatures, and exercise. Sanitation is also important, since a dirty cage is the perfect place for molds to grow. This is also the one area in which a bird can affect your health, since the dust and dander from birds, plus particles of dried bird feces, can cause respiratory problems in humans.

Egg Binding

Egg binding refers to a hen being unable to pass an egg. A common cause of this is a shell-less egg due to low levels of calcium in the diet. As the muscles squeeze down, instead of passing the egg, this merely compresses it. It can also be caused by weak muscles and other conditions, but most often is associated with poor diet and/or overbreeding. Many owners think this has nothing to do with a pet parrot, but that assumption is incorrect.

Unfortunately, a non-breeding pet bird occasionally does lay eggs. The irony here is that it is a good environment and diet that brings the bird into breeding condition, but, since the bird has no mate and no nest box, she will often continue to lay even if her owner does not remove the eggs. (Normally the hen lays until she has a clutch, then stops to incubate them.) This then brings about calcium exhaustion from excessive egg manufacture, and egg binding can occur.

An eggbound bird will be in obvious distress, usually at the

A variety of dangers are introduced when a parrot is taken outside— escape, injury, predators, accidents, etc.

bottom of the cage, relatively immobile. The vent area will be hard and swollen. First aid treatment is heat. Place the bird in a hospital cage—an empty aquarium with a heat lamp or a heating pad works in a pinch. With a valuable bird like a parrot, it is important to consult a veterinarian. There are many treatments the doctor may try, including injections. Unfortunately, egg binding tends to recur. You should seek and follow your veterinarian's advice for future prophylactic treatment.

Traveling Time and Outside Play

In many ways a parrot is like a child that does not grow up, so many people travel with their pet parrot. This is often the best solution to vacation concerns; if your parrot is with you, you know it is being cared for, and it will not be scared or lonely in your absence. Many of the hazards and concerns about traveling are also present when you take your pet outdoors for fresh air and play time in the sun.

Security

Your foremost concern should be the safety and security of your pet. Parrots are very prone to getting into trouble, and at the same time they are very valuable and subject to theft.

Escape

Do not believe that a tame bird, bonded to you, that always comes flying when you call, will not fly away from you. In an unfamiliar place a bird may take off out of fear or disorientation and simply fly hard. By the time it stops to try to get its bearings, it will be far from you and hopelessly lost. Please note that you do not have to be traveling for this to happen.

If you are in your backyard, where your parrot has gone many times, happily flying around and returning to you, it could bolt if a large dog, or a hawk, or a delivery truck, or a helicopter,

Even the most well-trained parrot may become frightened enough to fly away, before realizing that it is lost.

Taming and training outdoors should only be considered appropriate after a parrot's wings have been clipped.

or anything spooky comes along. There's more hope of getting it back than if it flies off in a bus terminal, but there is no guarantee.

Think a parrot won't fly off from its mate? Think again. You would not believe how often breeders advertise for a new mate for a parrot whose mate escaped and never looked back.

So, how do you protect yourself and your parrot? Simple: *Never take your parrot outside your home unless its wings are both clipped short.* Please note that I did not qualify this with exceptions based on cages, carriers, etc. Latches fail, cages fall apart, curious fingers open things. A well-clipped bird cannot fly off, and while it can still give you quite a chase, you're more likely to be able to get it back.

If your bird does fly off, or if it runs off into a crowd or climbs quickly out of sight somewhere, there are groups around the country that do their best to help find lost birds and to locate owners of found birds. A quick Internet search will turn up several you can contact.

Theft

A little common sense and forethought are your best weapons against someone stealing your bird. If you had to transport several stacks of $50 bills, would you place them in a transparent plastic box? Of course not. In public, your bird should be in a dark, cozy carrier *at all times.*

When at home, your bird should either be under observation or in a locked cage, and your home should be secure. Outside aviaries and cages are normally securely padlocked, but it is very easy for someone to enter an unlocked door or window and either grab or open a cage—especially professional bird thieves, who are knowledgeable about both robbery and parrots.

Your bird's band will help identify it if it is stolen, but bands can be cut off. If your bird is microchipped, it can always be identified, and although this does not protect it from being stolen, it increases the chances of recovery if it is.

A Survey of Parrot Species

I n this chapter, we'll look at a few of the many species of parrots you can consider as a pet. Each section will tell about a specific group of parrots (Amazons, macaws, etc.), and then there will be detailed descriptions of several representative species. We will cover many of the most commonly available birds, though you may find an excellent pet of a species not described here.

Technical note: Birds in general are notorious for occurring in a variety of subspecies and even distinct species in the natural state but freely interbreeding and hybridizing in captivity, and parrots are no exception. Sometimes the young are sterile, but often they are fertile, and their being used for breeding complicates things further. Very often different subspecies can be quite dissimilar—in size or in coloration, so mixing lineages can destroy some very distinct races of captive birds. The problem is, of course, that once gone there is no way to bring a variety back. Still, many aviculturalists become confused about the significance of subspecies versus species variation, and, to be sure, it is often a point of contention among taxonomists themselves.

Many people feel that we have a responsibility to preserve pure lineages of the natural variety, especially in the face of impending extinction in the wild for many types of birds. On the other hand, many people have delightful pets of hybrid origin. If you do not feel personally compromised by owning a hybrid bird, and if you find one that appeals to you, you will find its care to be the same as any purebred specimen.

Colorful, Comical Conure Clan

Conures are small to medium-sized large parrots, and in some people's minds, they sneak into this book on the tails of their larger cousins. Sometimes referred to as the poor person's macaws,

With so many colors, sizes, and personalities, the most difficult part about owning a parrot may be deciding which one to pick.

conures have many of the same characteristics but are much less expensive—by as much as a factor of ten.

Conures are the first of the three groups of neotropical parrots (New World) to be covered. There are several genera of conures, and they have close relationships to several other genera of mid-sized parrots, many of which make fine companion birds. Some individuals make fair talkers, mastering a few words, but they are known and loved more for their comical personalities than for any great talking ability.

Most conures are relatively inexpensive parrots. They reproduce more like parakeets than like large parrots, and they mature at a young age. They make an excellent first parrot, and they pack

Conures—such as these young jenday, nanday, and sun conures—are becoming increasingly popular as pets.

much of the appeal of the larger birds into a small and often colorful package. These playful clowns never cease to amaze their humans with the ingenuity and complexity of their tricks and acrobatics.

A medium-sized parrot cage is ample for these birds. They are not very large, but they are active and always appreciate more room. Toys such as ladders and swings are greatly appreciated by conures, and they will delight in inventing ways of playing with objects.

This group has no special dietary needs; a good diet with plenty of fresh fruits and vegetables is appropriate.

Taxonomic Relations

The jenday, gold-fronted, and gold-capped conures are variant subspecies that used to be separate species under the genus *Aratinga*. The most closely related conures are those of the genera that have been split from *Aratinga*, such as *Eupsittula, Nandayus,* and *Psittacara*. The extinct Carolina conure, *Conuropsis carolinensis*, looked uncannily like the sun conure. The genus *Pyrrhura* contains several conures that are notably smaller and quieter. These make wonderful pets and can even learn to say a few words, but they are definitely not large parrots.

Also closely related are the *Brotogeris* (canary-winged) parrots, and the *Pionites* or caiques. Although not rare, these birds are generally kept by advanced parrot breeders, though they have excellent pet qualities and are sure to become favorites as more people discover them.

Sun Conure

Aratinga solstitialis solstitialis

Native to: Northern Brazil

Size: About 12 inches

Color variations: The exact markings, especially the amount of red-orange coloration, are quite variable. Very often, the amount of "red" is much greater in young birds and disappears after the first molt, so it is usually unwise to pay extra for a "red sun." Hybridization with other subspecies increases the variability.

Availability: This species is very common in the hobby, and handfed babies are generally available.

Specific notes: One of the most popular conures, the sun is also one of the loudest. Not known for great talking ability, but some individuals do speak a bit. This is one of the most fun-loving and comical parrots, a truly acrobatic jokester. They are active and busy and will provide hours of interactive fun. "Playing dead" (laying on their back in your hand) is a favorite trick. If you can stand the noise, you will love the antics.

Sun Conure, Aratinga solsitialis solstitialis.

Jenday Conure

Aratinga solstitialis jandaya

Native to: Eastern Brazil

Size: About 12 inches

Color variations: This subspecies looks like a sun conure that had its colors coalesced—instead of splashes of green and red and yellow, the bird has a yellow head, red breast, green wings. Young birds may look more like suns.

Availability: This bird is quite common, almost as popular as the sun conure.

Specific notes: Behaviorally, the sun and the jenday are identical. The jenday is also an active clown, and it is equally noisy.

Dusky (-headed) Conure

Eupsittula weddellii

Native to: Western South America

Size: About 11 inches

Jenday Conure, Aratinga solstitialis jandaya.

Color variations: This parrot is green with a grayish-brown head.

Availability: This bird is fairly common in the trade, only slightly harder to find than nandays and suns.

Dusky Conure, Eupsittula weddelii.

Specific notes: This is yet another species that used to be classified in *Aratinga*; this conure looks most like the nanday.

If you want a conure but aren't sure you can take the noise, the dusky might be the solution. While it isn't silent by any means, it does not have the propensity for screeching that many conures do. They make great pets and can master a few words.

Nanday Conure

Nandayus nanday

Native to: Bolivia and Argentina

Size: About 12 inches

Color variations: This bird is basically green with a black face. The body shades to bluish on the underparts.

Availability: This species is extremely common in the hobby, and handfed babies are generally available.

Specific notes: Another popular and loud conure, with a typical piercing screech. Nandays are friendly and inquisitive by nature—even in the wild. They are also highly social, congregating in large flocks, sometimes with other species.

Majestic Macaws

Macaws are the gems of the rainforest, bringing the canopy to life with color, motion, and noise. They congregate in large flocks, intensifying both the sound and the rainbow beauty. Several macaw species are among the largest parrots, and since they have a long, "parakeet-like" tail, their overall length can top three feet. Not all macaws are big, and there are "mini" species the size of conures.

The bare white periophthalmic ring of the related conures becomes a bare patch in the macaws, and some species take bright coloration

Nanday Conure, Nandayus nanday.

to the extreme. A few of them are fairly cryptically colored in shades of green and blue, but several are colorful to the point of gaudiness. Consider the blue and gold macaw (aptly named) and the scarlet macaw (overall bright red with yellow and blue patches). Their coloration is alike only in that it is bright and contrastive in each case, yet these birds are able to hybridize and produce viable young, so they are obviously quite closely related.

Macaws have extremely powerful beaks that are able to effortlessly crack the toughest nuts, as well as to easily rip apart welded wire mesh, and the larger species need special cages to prevent escape. They give the impression of being top heavy, as if their heads are oversized. This appearance is due to the massive bill and the musculature that powers it. They can whittle a wooden perch to shavings in short order, and they must be allowed to chew to maintain their beaks. Destructible toys are perfect for these birds.

Cages for macaws must be large, and those for large macaws must be huge—and strongly built. The standard parrot diet should be supplemented with oily nuts such as Brazil nuts and walnuts; the birds have no trouble shelling such hard seeds.

Most specimens are fun loving and affectionate, but macaws have a tendency to become cranky, and it is important that you develop a relationship of mutual trust and respect from the start. You should never punish a parrot, but if you reinforce good behavior, they are smart enough to quickly get the idea of how they should behave. If you give a macaw the upper hand, they will take it. They like to have things their way, so your job is to convince them that your way is theirs also.

Many macaws make fine talkers, mastering a number of words and using them in appropriate

The macaws possess a wide range of spectacularly bright coloration patterns.

contexts. They are also popular subjects for trained and performing bird shows, since their spectacular appearance and great ability to learn tricks make them surefire winners.

Macaws are expensive. They take many years to mature, their reproductive rate is relatively low, and there are many single pets that are never paired as breeders in captivity. To balance this, however, they are extremely long lived, so acquiring a baby macaw means you have a pet for life. On this note, macaws often become one-person birds. Although a macaw may simply become a member of a human family, many form a very deep bond with a single human, and breaking them up can be traumatic for both. So, a macaw is not the best choice of a bird to get for a junior high student who will be off to college in a few years—just when the two of them have forged a mature relationship.

Taxonomic Relations

Macaws may be the most hybridized pet parrots. One reason has been the high price and limited availability of these birds. Someone with a male of one species and a female of another can breed them and produce saleable babies. This is generally not accepted as responsible breeding, but it is a fact of life that there are many hybrid

Consider the power and strength of a macaw's bill before deciding to own one as a pet; they are capable of great destruction.

macaws out there. There even are accepted names for the crosses, even for second generation and third generation hybrids such as the Catalina macaw (blue and gold x scarlet), the Camelot macaw (Catalina x scarlet), and the Capri macaw (Camelot x scarlet).

Macaws are most closely related to the conures, being in the same subfamily, Aratinginae. This subfamily includes the macaw genera *Ara, Anodorhynchus, Cyanospitta, Diopsittaca,* and various conure genera.

All of these birds share family status (Aratingidae) with the Amazons, caiques, and others.

Hyacinth Macaw

Anodorhynchus hyacinthinus

Native to: The interior of South America

Size: About 40 inches

Color variations: This is one of those birds that is breathtakingly beautiful in a single color. Except for the highlight of a yellow periophthalmic ring and a yellow band at the insertion point of the lower mandible, the hyacinth is overall a dazzling cobalt blue color.

Availability: This bird is *rare*. In the wild it is at or near extinction. Captive stocks are growing, but the demand far exceeds the supply. A proven breeding pair can cost $25,000 or more.

Hyacinth Macaw, Anodorhynchus hyacinthinus.
Photo courtesy of David Holzman, Palmforest Hyacinth Macaws, 5100 South Dixie Highway, Suite 13, West Palm Beach, FL 33405

Specific notes: Many believe that this bird should only be kept by serious breeders who will keep the birds in a responsible but ambitious breeding program. This is not to say all hyacinths should be parent raised—far from it. But even handfed pets should be part of a breeding effort to establish a viable captive population.

Greenwing Macaw, Ara chloroptera.

These birds are, however, excellent pets—probably the most docile of all macaws. Diligent breeding programs today can mean that future generations may enjoy readily available hyacinths.

Because this bird feeds naturally on palm nuts, it requires a diet higher in fats than most other parrots, even than other macaws.

Greenwing Macaw

Ara chloroptera

Native to: South America

Size: About 3 feet, very heavy bodied

Color variations: Similar to the scarlet, with the yellow band replaced by green, these birds are found with their overall red coloration of varying darkness. In some individuals it becomes a deep maroon.

Availability: This macaw is harder to find, though successful breeding programs are making more available. It is usually more expensive than the other large macaws.

Specific notes: This is a big and hefty macaw, but many find it the gentlest. It is notorious, however, for using its massive beak to destroy wire pens, as do the large cockatoos.

Scarlet Macaw, Ara macao.

Color variations: There is little variation, which is surprising, given its wide natural range, which often produces several subspecies.

Availability: If anything, the blue and gold is even more popular than the scarlet.

Specific notes: These big birds are known for being playful, and the sight of such a large parrot with an awesome beak cuddling like a baby is quite endearing.

Yellow-Collared Macaw

Ara auricollis

Native to: Central South America

Size: About 15 inches

Color variations: This is a handsome, dark green bird with a bright yellow "collar." The collar is generally more prominent in males.

Scarlet Macaw

Ara macao

Native to: Mexico to Brazil

Size: About 3 feet

Color variations: The major variation in this strikingly colored bird is in the amount (if any) of green mixed in with the yellow band on the wings.

Availability: This species is quite common, for a macaw.

Specific notes: This bird is certainly an eye-catcher, and it will prove an intelligent, if a bit temperamental, pet. While all of the large macaws require a special commitment, the scarlet is known for being quite moody and difficult.

Blue and Gold Macaw

Ara ararauna

Native to: South America

Size: About 3 feet

Blue and Gold Macaw, Ara araruna.

Availability: This little macaw is growing in popularity and availability.

Specific notes: These are highly social and very vocal birds that make good pets and are known for good talking ability.

Severe Macaw

Ara severa

Native to: Northern South America

Size: About 18 inches

Color variations: Although this bird is an overall green color, it has red and blue accents on its wings and tail. The two recognized subspecies differ mainly in size.

Availability: This is the most prevalent of the mini macaws.

Specific notes: Of the small species, this is perhaps the most like the larger macaws. It even has the tiny tracts of feathers creating lines in the bare white facial patch. This is a perfect choice if you want a lot of macaw in a small package.

Military Macaw

Ara militaris

Native to: Mexico into much of South America

Size: About 30 inches

Severe Macaw, Ara severa.

Military Macaw, Ara militaris.

Color variations: This macaw is overall green and blue, with red on the forehead; there is some variation in coloration, with the Bolivian subspecies showing a maroon throat.

Availability: The military macaw is quite common in the pet trade. The demand for them is not as great as for the splashier colored species, so the price for them is a bit lower.

Specific notes: This mid-sized macaw makes a nice compromise for someone who wants a large macaw but doesn't want to deal with the biggest species. Although not as colorful as the scarlet or blue and gold, the military makes as good or better a pet.

Hahn's (Noble) Macaw, Diopsitaca nobilis.

Hahn's (Noble) Macaw

Diopsittaca nobilis

Native to: Brazil

Size: 10 to 12 inches

Color variations: All subspecies are similar, with overall green plumage accented by red on the underside of the wings. The common names Hahn's and noble are applied inconsistently to the two major subspecies, *D. n. nobilis* and *D. n. cumanensis*, this latter being the larger race.

Availability: These charming birds are readily available.

Specific notes: This species is an excellent choice for a pet. Realize that with these mini macaws about half of the total length is tail, making them really diminutive. Its voice is also greatly reduced, so that it is unable to make quite the deafening din of its larger cousins.

Many ornithologists feel that this bird, the only member of its genus, is an intermediate between the macaws and the conures. Notice that the facial patch is larger than a conure's periophthalmic ring, but smaller than those of macaws of the genus *Ara*.

Amazing Amazons

Known to be among the best talkers, these large parrots are extremely popular. Their natural sounds are more a deep-throated clucking than a screech—almost like a very loud rusty hinge—and their speech often has that strained-voiced sound of the stereotypical "Polly wanna cracker" type. Many of them become accomplished singers, whistlers, and talkers, and they normally seem to understand the meaning of what they say and enter into mini conversations with people. The double yellow head and blue front are especially noted for their talking ability.

This third group of neotropical parrots consists of a single genus with many species. All of the Amazons are closely related and similar in appearance. They are overall green, often with black lacing on the feathers, and they typically sport some bright colors—red, blue, yellow—somewhere on their body. These

Through predominantly green in color, the Amazons are attractive and talented birds that make great pets.

color accents are usually found on the wings and the head. Even within a single species there is considerable variation in the intensity and extent of these colorations.

Amazons are large. While their total length is not much more than many conures, very little of that length is due to tail, and they are hefty birds. Amazons are relatively quiet and sedate (for parrots), but they are not averse to acrobatic fun and games, and they greet dawn, dusk, and other excitements with a respectably parrot-like vociferousness. They are very intelligent and will definitely interact with you. Behaviorally, they are quite similar to African Greys.

The personality of Amazons is a bit aloof and independent. Tame pets are quite affectionate—when they want to be. If you like a cat's independence, you'll appreciate an Amazon's occasional need for personal space and time. Like all parrots, they need a lot of attention and time spent with them, but unlike cockatoos, for example, they usually don't feel they need *all* of your time.

Price-wise, Amazons are right in the middle—higher than the conures, less than the macaws and cockatoos.

Taxonomic Relations

Most of the other genera in the subfamily Amazoninae are rare in the pet trade, except for the genus *Pionus*. This is a large group of colorful parrots. The various species occur from Central America through most of South America. Handfed birds make very interesting pets, and they will undoubtedly become even more popular as breeding programs increase.

Orange-Winged Amazon

Amazona amazonica

Native to: Northern South America

Size: About 12 inches, one of the smaller Amazons

Color variations: The standard Amazon green is supplemented in this species with a yellow face and a bluish forehead. Appropriately, there are reddish-orange flight feathers.

Availability: This species is very commonly available as breeders, but it's somewhat harder to find an orange-winged handfed baby than, say, a blue front.

Specific notes: A small but otherwise typical Amazon, the orange wing is not known for special talking ability, though it often develops into quite a mimic. It can be very noisy, however.

Yellow-Headed Amazon

Amazona ochrocephala

Native to: Southern Central America and northern South America

Size: About 14 to 16 inches

Color variations: The various subspecies differ mostly in the amount of yellow on the head. Common names for these races include yellow-headed, yellow-crowned, yellow-front-ed, Panama yellow-headed, and others.

Yellow-Headed Amazon, Amazona ochrocephala.

Availability: This bird is commonly available.

Specific notes: This species once contained six subspecies, but two have been elevated to species status, *A. auropalliata* and *A. oratrix.*

This and related species are intelligent, friendly, vocal birds, with varying but often excellent talking abilities.

Double Yellow-Headed Amazon

Amazona oratrix

Native to: Southern Mexico and northern Central America

Size: About 14 inches

Color variations: The unsuitability of common names is evident with this species. Although the Tres Marias subspecies (A. o. tresmariae) has a completely yellow head, other subspecies may have yellow only on the upper parts of the head. The red on the bend of the wing is usually prominent.

Availability: This is a very popular and commonly available Amazon.

Specific notes: It is easy to see why the taxonomy of these birds has such a changeable history. Even within a subspecies there is individual variation in the yellow coloration, and many captive-bred specimens are hybrids among the subspecies, even further complicating identification.

Double Yellow-Headed Amazon, Amazona oratrix.

Many people claim this is the best talker among the Amazons. While you are unlikely to get orations from your bird, it will likely prove a ready mimic. These birds are also known as being tame and gentle, so their striking coloration, talking ability, and personality make them a triple-winner as a pet.

Blue-Fronted Amazon

Amazona aestiva

Native to: Eastern Brazil

Size: About 15 inches

Color variations: As with most Amazons, the exact coloration is quite variable, especially in the amount of blue and yellow in the face. The red shoulder is typical. The green feathers are often laced with black.

One subspecies, often called the yellow-winged Amazon, has extensive yellow coloration on the wings, even extending into the neck and body.

Blue-Fronted Amazon, Amazona aestiva.

Availability: The blue-fronted Amazon is one of the most popular Amazons and is regularly available.

Specific notes: This is a typical Amazon, and usually a good talker. In the wild this species frequently flocks with other Amazon parrots, and pet Amazons of different species usually get along quite well together.

Yellow-Naped Amazon

Amazona auropalliata

Native to: Southern Mexico, Nicaragua, Honduras

Size: About 14 inches

Color variations: The yellow-naped (subspecies *A. a. auropalliata*) and the parviceps (subspecies *A. a. parviceps*) differ a bit in size, and the parviceps has red on the wing. The size and extent of the yellow splotch on the back of the neck can vary a bit.

Availability: This species is not quite as common as the blue front but is readily available.

Specific notes: The taxonomy of the yellow-on-the-head Amazons has undergone considerable upheaval. This bird was elevated to species status after initially being considered a subspecies of *A. ochrocephala,* as was the double yellow head, *A. oratrix.* All of these Amazons are threatened in the wild due to illegal poaching and habitat loss, but captive-bred specimens are common.

Yellow-Naped Amazon, Amazona auropalliata.

Garrulous Greys

In almost every way, the African Grey parrot is the quintessential parrot. This is the parrot one imagines riding on a pirate's shoulder, and this is the parrot that has, through the research of Dr. Irene Pepperberg and the accomplishments of her friend Alex (an African Grey), brought the intelligence and communicative skills of parrots to the attention of the scientific community.

Greys, Greys, Greys

All Greys are the same species, *Psittacus erithacus.* There are at least two subspecies, with certain populations extinct or near extinct in the wild. Ready breeders, there are plenty of captive-bred Greys available, and no birds should ever be trapped for the pet trade.

Plus Poicephalus

The genus *Poicephalus* is the only other genus in the subfamily Psittacinae. There are many species in this genus, but the most common pet among them is the perky Senegal. While gray is a common color for this genus, it is not an overall coloration as with the African Grey—in fact, the tiny Senegal looks like a miniature Grey whose body (but not its head) got colored green and orange. It acts like a miniature Grey as well, even using its feet to manipulate toys.

Other Taxonomic Relations

The family Psittacidae has one other subfamily, Coracopinae, to which the vasa parrots belong (genus *Coracopsis*). Like many animal residents of Madagascar, these birds are rare and endangered. They are also rather odd, exhibiting many primitive parrot characteristics. They are not usually found in the pet trade, though some captive breeding is occurring.

Congo African Grey

Psittacus erithacus erithacus

Native to: Central Africa

Size: 14 to 15 inches

Color variations: The overall gray coloration is accented by white feathers on the face and red tail feathers. Red feathers elsewhere on the body are common.

Congo African Grey, Psittacus erithacus.

Availability: This bird is increasingly common and available, and the price has been decreasing for some time due to very successful captive breeding programs.

Specific notes: Few people dispute the Grey's prominence among talking parrots. Handfed birds are much more family members than pets, though they sometimes develop fierce one-on-one bonds with a single human. They are highly intelligent and must be given creative outlets.

Timneh African Grey, Psittacus erithacus timneh.

Timneh African Grey

Psittacus erithacus timneh

Native to: Western Africa

Size: 12 to 13 inches

Color variations: This subspecies is usually darker than the Congo Grey, and the red on the tail is more maroon.

Availability: The Timneh is also common, and it usually costs a little less than the larger Congo.

Specific notes: Aside from size and depth of color, the two are the same. Either one makes an excellent, intelligent, and talkative pet.

Senegal Parrot

Poicephalus senegalus

Native to: Senegal and surrounding African nations

Size: About 9 inches

Color variations: This is a green bird with a gray head and color on the belly. This color varies from yellow through orange to a red-orange. The green breast forms a V between the orange sides.

Senegal Parrot, Piocephalus senegalus.

Availability: This bird is very common and is much less expensive than the related Greys.

Specific notes: If you want an African Grey but don't have the room or money to get one, the little Senegal is a good alternative. These colorful and friendly birds are not much bigger than a lovebird, but behaviorally, they are big parrots. They make good talkers and are extremely affectionate. This is definitely the "apartment-size" parrot.

Captivating Cockatoos

Cockatoos are unusual. They fascinate us with their differences from other parrots. Their powdery soft, luxurious plumage and subtle color schemes are gorgeous—gone are the greens and the flashy reds and blues of other parrots, replaced instead by off-whites and grays and pastel washes. Their crests, which are often highlighted with color, raise and lower expressively and seem to make up for a bird's lack of real facial expressions. Their heavy bills can crack nuts you'd need a hammer and chisel to open, but they can also deftly and delicately hull the tiniest seeds. Their raucous voices can rattle your eardrums, but they can also imitate both noises and human speech so uncannily that they can fool you into answering the doorbell or checking to see what the dog is barking about. These birds are playful, very intelligent, and affectionate to the extreme. Many love to be held and cuddled like a baby, and they refuse to be ignored when they want attention, which is most of the time.

Although generally not as colorful as some other parrots, the cockatoos have much to offer in the way of dramatic crest displays and personality.

In the pet trade, most species are of the genus *Cacatua*, including the umbrella, sulphur-crested, Goffin's, and Moluccan. These white birds can be sexed by eye color—the male's iris is dark brown or black, and the female's is reddish.

"Terrible 'Toos"

If parrots are toddlers, then cockatoos represent the Terrible Twos phase. They are petulant and prone to tantrums if they feel they are not getting sufficient attention from their humans. But, they are also the cuddliest, snuggliest babies, and absolutely irresistible. Even though acquiring any parrot requires a substantial commitment, the cockatoos take this to the extreme. They give back as much as they take, however, and they will shower you with love and attention, they will learn to speak, and they will bond themselves to you as tightly as a doting puppy.

This bond can be so strong that the bird will suffer severe trauma if its life is uprooted. These birds cannot be purchased on a whim and then left in a cage after the excitement is over. They will become screamers and self-pluckers and worse. It is important to socialize baby cockatoos to many different people and situations so that they will not react adversely when confronted with different situations when they are older.

Taxonomic Relations

The cockatoos are an isolated group in the order Psittaciformes. Their family Cacatuidae contains only two subfamilies, Cacatuinae, which contains all of the cockatoo genera, and the not-too-closely-related Nymphicinae, which contains the lone genus *Nymphicus*, with the single species *hollandicus*, the cockatiel.

In the subfamily Cacatuinae are the white cockatoos (genus *Cacatua*), the galah or rose-breasted cockatoo (genus *Eolophus*), and the gang-gang and large black cockatoos, which are all very rare and not commonly encountered as pets. These large birds (almost as long as macaws, but with much shorter tails) are best located in serious breeding programs.

Goffin's Cockatoo

Cacatua goffini

Native to: Indonesia

Size: 12 to 13 inches

Color variations: This bird is white, with pale yellow underparts.

Availability: This is probably the most commonly available cockatoo, and one of the most reasonably priced.

Specific notes: This small 'too is a real snuggle bug. Although it is small in size, and small crested, it has a loud voice, and it is not averse to using it to get attention. They are very intelligent, gentle, and affectionate.

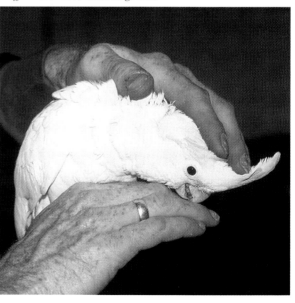

Goffin's Cockatoo, Cacatua goffini.

Leadbeater's (Major Mitchell's) Cockatoo

Cacatua leadbeateri

Native to: Australia

Size: About 15 inches

Color variations: This bird is a study in pink pastel. A pink head and breast complement its overall white body, and the crest, which bends slightly forward, has bands of dark pink, yellow, and white.

Availability: Very rare, very expensive.

Specific notes: This is not the best species for a pet parrot. First of all, they are shy and easily upset; although some owners enjoy their personality, they are not at all like most other cockatoos. Second, they are rare both in captivity and in the wild, and captive birds should be in breeding programs. Unfortunately, they are extremely difficult to breed.

Leadbeater's (Major Mitchell's) Cockatoo, Cacatua leadbeateri.

Umbrella (White-Crested) Cockatoo, Cacatua alba.

Umbrella (White-Crested) Cockatoo

Cacatua alba

Native to: Indonesia

Size: About 18 inches

Color variations: The umbrella is 100 percent white, though there is a hint of yellow under the wings and tail.

Availability: This is a very popular cockatoo, about as common as the Goffin's.

Specific notes: The huge white crest is this species' most distinctive feature and gives it its common name. These birds make friendly and intelligent pets. They have a loud voice, but they don't seem to use it as much as some other cockatoos.

Greater Sulfur-Crested Cockatoo

Cacatua galerita

Native to: Indonesia, Australia, New Guinea

Size: About 20 inches

Greater Sulfur-Crested Cockatoo, Cacatua galerita.

Color variations: Basically a white bird with a yellow crest. There are several subspecies, as is common in a bird with such a wide distribution. The triton cockatoo has a bluish eye ring, which is white in the other subspecies.

Availability: For a cockatoo, this species is quite common, which means it is difficult but not impossible to find.

Specific notes: This large cockatoo is always a favorite. It makes a good talker and an affectionate pet.

Lesser Sulfur-Crested Cockatoo

Cacatua sulphurea
Native to: Indonesia
Size: About 13 inches
Color variations: The overall white is complemented in this species by yellow highlights—in the crest and under the wings and tail. There is a yellow cheek spot reminiscent of the cockatiel's orange cheek spot.

The yellow is replaced by orange in the citron-crested subspecies.

Availability: This species is relatively common in the trade, but quite expensive.

Specific notes: This bird is a typical loud cockatoo. Usually a fairly good talker, it is also adept at learning tricks.

Rose-Breasted Cockatoo

Eolophus roseicapillus
Native to: Australia
Size: 12 to 14 inches
Color variations: This subtly beautiful bird has a soft pink body, gray wings, and white crest.

Availability: So common in its homeland of Australia that it is sometimes an agricultural pest, this species is rare in aviculture in the United States and commands a very high price.

Specific notes: Most specimens are in breeding programs, though pet owners find this bird makes a fine pet—extroverted to the point of bossiness.

Rose-Breasted Cockatoo, Eolophus roseicapillus.

Moluccan Cockatoo

Cacatua moluccensis

Native to: Indonesia (Moluccan Islands)

Size: About 22 inches

Color variations: The plumage varies from white to white with a salmon-pink wash. The crest is pink. Some specimens are extremely pink.

Availability: A very popular bird, this species is fairly common but quite expensive.

Specific notes: These birds are known for their affectionate nature and for their talking ability. They are very popular as pets.

Elegant Eclectus

The eclectus is the only species in its genus, but there are several regional variants, largely due to its island habitat. The most common in the hobby are the vos (vosmaeri), the Solomon Island, and the red-sided, which itself comprises several subspecies. Although breeders make an effort to keep the subspecies pure, there are quite a few hybrids around. Of course, such birds have nothing wrong with them and make fine pets. The only concern in mixing the subspecies is that if and when the day comes that there are no more wild populations, it would be very nice to still have the original subspecies intact in captivity.

These are gentle, intelligent, and colorful birds, known for their sweet personalities. They are usually good mimics, and they have an unusual repertoire of natural vocalizations, including metallic noises and other strange calls.

Taxonomic Relations

They belong to the family Psittaculidae, whose name implies "little parrots," but they are large birds—over a foot long, with a small tail. The familiar short-tailed lovebirds of the genus *Agapornis* and the highly domesticated, very long-tailed Indian ring-necked parrots of the genus *Psittacula* are undoubtedly the best-known members of this family. Though

Moluccan Cockatoo, Cacatua moluccensis.

The Eclectus Parrots are extremely colorful birds that make intelligent and gentle companions.

nowhere near as prevalent as these small, colorful parrots, eclectus parrots are firmly established in aviculture. The rest of the family, however, and it is a large one with many different genera, is poorly represented in captive stocks.

Obvious Others

Perfect Parakeets

The Australian region is the natural home for many other hookbill species that are popular in aviculture. The most prevalent are the broad-tails, especially the rosellas, and the Australian grass parakeets, including the Bourke's, splendid, and elegant parakeets.

Included here by personality would be the extremely popular cockatiel, which is the "parakeet" of the cockatoo family.

All of these birds are smaller, more common, and less expensive than larger parrots, and they may not have the same intelligence, talking ability, or interactive personalities. Handfed specimens, however, make loving pets, can learn tricks, and can even speak a little.

Lovebirds are among the smaller parrots that are incredibly popular with beginners.

Lovable Lories

The lories are another popular group in the trade. These are highly, often spectacularly, colored birds. Their specialized diet is based in the wild on feeding on flowers and fruits, and they therefore have very unusual tongues and beaks. Again, these can make wonderful pets, even if not of the same type as the large parrots.

Marvelous Minis

I've already pointed out the tiny Senegal that is small in size but acts like a large parrot. There are many small parrots, however, that differ substantially from large parrots in both appearance and behavior, as well as in size. These birds can make excellent pets, and some even learn to squeak out a word or two. Included in this group are the African lovebirds, genus *Agapornis,* and the South American parrotlets of the genus *Forpus.* These birds are real characters. Handfed individuals are fearless and affectionate, and they don't seem to realize just how small they are! They make fascinating and lovable pets in their own right.

These tiny and inexpensive members of the vast variety of parrot species make excellent first birds, and they serve well to introduce young and old to the pleasures of owning a companion bird without the expense and commitment required for their larger cousins.